FAMILY MATTERS: HOMAGE TO JULY, THE SLAVE GIRL

Jeff
30 Sept 2008
From
pat

FAMILY MATTERS: HOMAGE TO JULY, THE SLAVE GIRL

Shelby Stephenson

Bellday Books, Inc.

Durham, North Carolina and Pittsburgh, Pennsylvania

Published by Bellday Books, Inc., P.O. Box 3687, Pittsburgh, PA 15230
www.belldaybooks.com

ACKNOWLEDGEMENTS
Grateful acknowledgment to the editors of the following publications, in which versions of these poems first appeared: *Aires One, Benson Review, Bits, Blackjack Twelve: Step Around the Mountain: Southern Appalachian Mountains, Bone & Flesh, Caesura, Cairn, Crab Creek Review, Crucible, A Gathering At the Forks: Fifteen Years of the Hindman Settlement School, Appalachian Writers' Workshop, Hawk & Whippoorwill Recalled, Here's To the Land: A Celebration of 60 Years By the NC Poetry Society, I Have Walked: Stories and Poems About Poverty, Journal of North Carolina-Virginia College English Association, Kansas Quarterly, Kentucky Poetry Review, Long Shot, Lonzie's Fried Chicken, The Lyricist, The Manhattan Review, North Carolina Humanities, North Carolinians Write About Poverty, The Olive Branch, Onionhead Literary Quarterly, The Panhandler, Pembroke Magazine, The Pilot: Southern Accent, Pine Straw: The Magazine of Life Art & Entertainment in the Sandhills, Potato Eyes, Poetry Under the Stars, The Richmond Reader, The Sandhills Review, Scripsit, A Sense of Place, Sisyphus, The Smithfield Herald, Solo Cafe 2: Oppression & Forgiveness: A Journal of Poetry, The Sow's Ear, The Spoon River Quarterly, Tabula Rasa, This End Up Postcard, A Time to Listen: An Anthology of Regional Poets, Turning Dances: An Anthology of North Carolina Poets, Turnstile, Twigs, Washout Review, Wellspring, The White Pelican Review, Wolfpen Branch.* Section VIII of "Playing Off One Another" first appeared as "Work" in *Broadside* published by Leverette T. Smith, Jr., North Carolina Wesleyan College Press: version of section III of "Your Name Is July" first appeared as "The Past," a Broadside published by Jeffery Beam at Golgonooza at Frog Level, Hillsborough, North Carolina, and as part of "The South" in a chapbook, *Greatest Hits*, published by Pudding House. Versions of sections I and II of "The Roll Call Of Tenants" first appeared in *Carolina Shout!* (Playwright's Fund of North Carolina) and *Fiddledeedee* (The Bunny & the Crocodile Press). Versions of parts of *Family Matters: Homage to July, The Slave Girl* came out in a chapbook, *Poor People*, published by Night Shade Press.

Cover and interior design by Cassandra Patten.

Library of Congress Cataloguing-in-Publication Data

Stephenson, Shelby, 1938
       Family Matters: Homage To July, The Slave Girl / Shelby Stephenson.
         p. cm.

    ISBN 978-0-9793376-1-1

1. Americans-Poetry. I. Title.
Library of Congress Control Number 2008934702

For Nin

FAMILY MATTERS: HOMAGE TO JULY, THE SLAVE GIRL
Table of Contents

State of North Carolina
Johnston County

Know all men by these presents that I, George Stephenson, Guardian of the Heirs of Jacob T. Woodall, deceased of Johnston County and State of North Carolina, in consideration of the sum of Four hundred and thirteen dollars and twenty-five cents to me in hand paid by Seth Woodall of the County and State aforesaid, the receipt of which is hereby fully acknowledged, have granted, bargained and Sold and by these presents do bargain, grant, Sell and Convey unto the said Seth Woodall a certain negro Girl a Slave named July about 10 years old.

To Have and to hold the same the said Seth Woodall, his Heirs, Executors, Administrators and assigns forever free and discharged of any and all encumbrances whatsoever and for the better security of the title hereby conveyed I for myself, my heirs, Executors and Administrators to and with the said Seth Woodall, his heirs, Executors, Administrators and assigns do warrant and forever defend the same from the lawful claim of any and all persons whatever. In testimony whereof I hereunto set my hand and seal, this 11th day of Jan. 1850.

George Stephenson {Seal}

Signed, Sealed and
delivered in presence of
Gideon Woodall
William Woodall

Johnston County Court
February Term, 1851.

When was the due execution of this deed duly acknowledged in open Court by the Grantor and ordered to be Registered–
Thomas Bagley, Clerk.

-Johnston County Deeds Book, W-2, pp. 114-115, Microfilm, State Archives, Raleigh, North Carolina

Your Name Is July

I

Your name is July—
there is no record I know about
beyond the account of your sale.

Did you know your place
and my greatgreatgranddad's too?

Rummaging around the homeplace,
pronouncing your name *Ju-ly*,
I hear my father—*This land will be yours someday*—

what graveyard of bones—
mounds and stones,
the "I owned"—
you there, Jart, Venus, Silvy, Clay.
April's wildflowers run at your feet.
Did winters fill your shoes with snow?

Pap George did live here.
The old washhouse still stands.

I kick the dust out of these fields.

II

Greatgreatgrandpap George's anvil
fits right between your shoulderblades.
The money used to buy and sell you
presses into my heart—

I remember—
never eating with "them."

"They" lived on "our place,"
my father's boyhood home,
  his father's homeplace;

4

they slept in the same rooms he grew up in.
So when they came to our shanty
my mother would fix
some plates to take to the porch;
we would talk through the screen;
they would eat their peas and fatback
and my mother took pride in
knowing they liked her food.

III

Chattelrattle downchute to market,
limbs swinging, nostrils flaring blood.
May streams and woods your vestments be,
your creeks fill with fish—
fields score with mercy.

Tenant shanties wear the landscape.
The graveyard moves the rip of the whip.

Monuments—unheard, still.
Fieldrocks grow moss and grieving.
Memory comes closer to mercy, uncompromising,
like medicine we take, wait.
Your warm color line never dies.
Fingers wave from galleys,
ships pushing through hell to bring us here.

Seven

*–Valuation of GEORGE STEPHENSON'S SLAVES in Johnston District,
According to the Decree passed by county board on the first Thursday of April 1863:*

Names	Age	Class	Valuation	Remarks
Geraret	60	11	$ 130	
Venus	51	10	200	
Silvy	35	10	200	
Daniel	12	3	650	
Haywood	11	3	650	
Sarah	7	6	400	
Marzilla	6	6	400	
			$2,650.00	

Silvy totes a little water.
Sarah touches your handprints
branching boughs,
mouths your name, "Ju-ly,"
softening acres of cottonpatches; oxen–
out of yoke–nuzzle Sarah's shoulders.

Is that Daniel readying the sliding balances of a weighhorse,
a big pea and a little one, eyes round as bolls, a $650.00 pricetag?
Is that Haywood loading his wagon, pitchforking George's name?

Geraret mounts the mule and leads the sheep beside the hill.
Venus picks purplehulled fieldpeas.

Marzilla's blood leads her way though at six she cannot shed more to amount to much–
I hear you say: *The Big Man could skin us alive.*

One Still Worm & Cap

*   *–8 May 1845: David Stephenson of Johnston County to George Stephenson of Johnston County for natural love & affection to my son: horses, sheep, 1 still worm & cap, farming utensils & household furniture, excepting a lifetime right of David Stephenson, Sr., & wife Arey. . .Wit: Walter R. Moore, David (O) Stephenson.*
      Nov. Ct. 1845. Deed Bk. U-2 (Kinfolks of Johnston County: Abstracts of Deeds, 1826-1865, E. Ross and Z. Wood, Volume II, 90).

I

The still's crafted from copper,
the copper molded by a wooden mallet,
furnace, creekrocks, chinked with clay from Paul's Hill,

the cornmeal soaked in hotwater in the still,
the sun in summer, a cooker; in winter, the tub, fired.
In a little less than a week the corn malts.

Adding raw meal
David fills barrels one by one.
If the mash's too thick he adds water,
leaving the capped barrels to ferment all night.

Beer works the next day.
George mixes contents back and forth,
the whiskey and beer coming off at the same time.
In about a week, the cap, foamy,
as the alcohol eats it, comes clean.

Father and son pour the beer in the still, stoke the furnace.
The brew boils, the arm
tightening on the still's top, sealed with ryepaste.

July: *I hear the steam dancing through the arm to the worm,*
copper one, inside a barrel brimming with springwater.
The drippling liquor hummmmmnnnnns *the tub.*

Whiskey's everywhere–ditches, bushes, cornfields–
         apple, peach, banana, corn, scuppernong, tomato, grape.
I stamp them big, juicy Concords with my feet.
Nighttime's a scrabble.
I close my eyes and hear the Freedom Bell.
Then the sound really comes. I know what I will do.

II

1865:
In the pasture the jackass brays his teeth need briars to saw.
A cutaway scratches clods, blinks toads under spikes.
Mules pull a twohorse plow.
Tender nostrils deepen pails.

The chorusing dogs chase the horn.
Bells charm cows and chime the pasture's every cuddled tongue.
Vines trumpet lines.
Evenings flicker the clearpitched entablature of old commandments.

Dear July

–Charles Parrish & Tobitha Dodd of Johnston County sell
(29 May 1830) to Ephriam Ferrell of Johnston County 4 negroes–woman Winney ca.
24 yrs., boy Henry ca. 5 yrs., boy Nedom ca. 3 yrs. & girl July ca. 6 mos.
Wit: Isaac Stallings. Signed Charles (E) Parrish, Tobitha (X) Dodd, Aug. Ct. 1832
(Kinfolks, Vol. II, 29).

I am the thrill and taint of the Durham Tobacco Market,
buyer's sweat, auctioneer's chant, the money.
You are the wornout sunsuits, the cattymount squatted in Beaver Dam,
the throwedaways and the sailing ships the slave galleys barnacle.

I hitch up the plow, bear down on the handles as I
pass the Nimrod Stephenson Memorial Cemetery,

no names on many stones, the graveyard an old field:
Here we are, you say, your season's turning fall,
as mid-summer's seven to nine September winds.
It's a long while from slavery times to now, though no more than a winter's day,

the dancing bobbers floating from the bank in and out of
tide's remembrance on Middle Creek where you and Clay sit on fertilizer sacks.

Separate Equals

–AFRICAN AMERICAN SCHOOLS IN JOHNSTON COUNTY IN THE 1920's:
Atkinson's Academy, Bethel, Booker Washington, Cedar Grove, Four Oaks, Green,
Hodges Chapel, Long Branch, Micro, Montgomery, New Bethel, Pine Level, Pineville,
Piney Grove, Princeton, Ransom's Academy, Rocky Branch, St. Amanda, Simms, Stewart,
Stony Hill, Union, Watson, Wilson's Mills (Compiled, Margaret McLemore Lee,
Johnston County Heritage Center, Smithfield, N. C.).

–SCHOOLS OF JOHNSTON COUNTY (WHITE)–ca. 1921–ca. 1930:
Allen, Archer Lodge, Bagley, Banner, Baptist Center, Barbour, Barnes, Batten,
Beasley Grove, Blacksman, Boyette, Brown, Clayton, Corbett, Corbett-Hatcher, Corinth,
Creech, Elevation, Emit, Four Oaks, Glendale, Glenwood, Grove, Hales, Hatcher,
Holly Grove, Jernigan Grove, Jerome, Johnson, Hickory, Hightower, Holders, Live Oak, Lon
Pines, Massey, Meadow, Mill Creek, Moore, Mount Zion, New Beulah, Niagara,
Oak Grove, Ogburn, Oliver, Parker, Pierce, Pine Level, Pineville, Piney Grove, Pittman,
Plain View, Pleasant Grove, Pleasant Hill, Polenta, Poplar Grove, Poplar Springs,
Powhatan, Princeton, Rehobeth, Rock Hill, Royal, Royall, Sandy Grove, Sandy Ridge,
Sandy Springs, Selma, Shiloh, Smith, Smithfield, Spilona, Stanley, Steward, Stilley,
Sunny Nook, Temple Hill, Thanksgiving, Thornton, Wildwood, Wilson's Mills, Yelvington
Grove, Zebulon (As listed by H. B. Marrow, Johnston County Heritage Center).

A slip came to the teacher's room—*Invitation to Join the Orpheus Boys Choir.*
We sang at Elizabeth Church (seats in the loft for the slaves).
We went to Fayetteville to sing on the radio.
We rode around the Old Slave Market, twice, on the way home.

The Candy Man

I

Came with his punchboard.
I pushed out numbers for choice prizes.
Once a month the promise went out over the countryside.
The Watkins Products Man, too.
Had a chicken coop tied to his front bumper.
He'd take a chicken as payment, say, for horse lineament.

Did you work to satisfy your credit at Pap's commissary,
       tense up when you entered the store?
Did the farmers there court the drinkstand to give you room?
Did you ever punch a board or trade eggs for pretty things?

I did have a Candy Man.
I did not wish for hair to let down to dry his feet at footwashings.
Sometimes I gave him an eyeful and lost him.
In the fall when colors called my face shadowed his window.
At dusk, the table set with fatback and molasses – his skin twinged until a voice
      sang for me alone until the tune went out of hearing.

II

Mr. Charlie Parrish's Store loomed way up Paul's Hill.
I would walk with eggs in my pockets to swap for merchandise,
      lean against the colddrinkbox and listen:

Hallo! Heck, I garn-dam-tee
you this: no ragged-assed farmer'll
get in no field today; tractors'll
mar up over the mufflers, I tell you –
row a boat in the ditches down yonder by Paul Coats's sloughs.

Tom's Roasted Peanuts float in a Pepsi Heck guzzles.
He's no holier-than-the-learned race of farmers who'll tell you:
Workworkwork and what do you get?!
Bonier and bonier and sloppy-assed in debt!
Sleeves waving, he lowers himself down the sandy, shackly, wooden steps.

11

"Memory believes before knowing remembers"

—William Faulkner, *Light In August*

I

Your story, July, sticks in my throat:
violence splits the syllables down a back road,
the smell of horsesweat, leather
creaking in the gee and haw of tongue and trace,
lightning bugs dancing on Percy's wagon,
his hat, the hole in the crown, pulled down,
bobbing, while the slow mules
go on up the hill
where he will "carry the truckrow," his hindend facing the sun,
the mule, humbling and humoring toward the shade,
the end, the beginning, a piece, fabric
cut from the sweat—the rows topped,
middles swamped with rotten blooms,
greenblack juices, splattered tobacco worms—
and Percy barely moving the truckrow,
a frail man bloated with jagged currents,
little rivulets his pores spilling.

II

Percy moves across the yard
to get the knife
to sling the weeds.
You chase the bees
to the tops of blooms
now laid low
not one left
to kick about like a mule's
flopped ears.
Would the missus looking from the window
say while the man rakes in piles
his day's work—

there—slave's work, after all?
I see you there,
your comfort uncomfortably
stationed at the master's door;
your wound in the landlord's side
coming through the blooming sounds
brought on by going from field to field for somebody else,
never for yourself
nor your children I know about, their shrill hunger
mornings when the doorknob was cold,
the hearth cold, floor cold.

Percy didn't have a cow
Percy didn't have a mule
Percy didn't have a hog

he would split stovewood
tossing each stick aside with his bandaged thumb
rubbing his bloodshot eyes with the back of his chopping hand.

Worked his tail to the bone,
told skinny tales
and Minnie was his
fosterdaughter, July, motherdaughterchildwife!

III

Considering how Minnie Birch picked the plantbed, those dime-sized tobacco
leaves pushing the canvas in April, it's so quick, don't you think, squatting on her knees,
using a spoonhandle to pinch out the morning glory and mullein, the grass, of course,
the worst part of the job, since it is everywhere, all months, alive or dead. *"Minnie, is your
Hard Rock growing?" "Like a weed!"* Snuff ages her lower lip like a promise the father
might dart around the corner and light up the path like a horn blowing—*who could bear
such news?* Minnie stares at July, not even wondering (or caring).

IV

A field full of Hands trudge up at dinnertime, desperate from heat and lack of water, the
bench where the tobacco is being prepared for the barn a din of wonder. The Help hums
"Amazing Grace." The men and women from the field seem hotter than ever, their
gummy clothes clinging to their bodies, feet black with sweat. Nearby: dirtroad, shack,
some tarpaper: inside, a big woman, nearly blind, says how her time has come: though
she needs plenty, she does not need money now: "Where is July? If I only had her to
talk to, cook for me, help me along, sing me a song."

V

You turn back the canvas
and squat with a brokenoff spoon
to dig the weeds,
tiny as fleas,
around the tobacco plants
the size of dimes.

Percy knots the canvas,
one long snake of plantbed covering,
places it top the tobacco racks.
Bench Help hums:
The tobacco's being tied on sticks stuck in wooden horses.

VI

You and Mae Dinah hoe the sheepburrweeds
out of the corn—"Makes it greener," Mae Dinah says,
"but I don't know if I can last—with my Elvis tired,
Lord, just plain tired down on his *feets*."

Hallie Sanders looks down at the cotton on the sheet, wondering after this one
and that one, the one on the weighhorse, given up as offering: "Mister Paul, you
got some more work I can do?"

Hallie's brother, Algie, wants to become a boxer like Joe Louis,
Daddy ordering some gloves from Sears-Roebuck,

drawing a ring in the pasture
and Bud, nicknamed Little One,
comes down from Mr. Hector's where he works and beats
Algie who has prepared for his bout
shadowboxing pines bobbing and weaving
and Little One pounds his face so good and hard
Algie pulls at the swells on his face for days
Little One's friend who comes with him to referee
down on his hands and knees
outside the scrawled circle, flapping the dirt with his palms
saying *Little One done whupped him Little One*

Buddy Dublin streaks the countryside in a SoupedUp
Cadillac Coupe de Ville: *My daddy's a leatherskinned wampus cat*
they call Pearl . . . my mama's a miracle whelped in hell and I am Dublin–

Buddy's my name–I can whup any man–love a woman to shame! Mauling a wedge
sinking into trees he centers cordwood for woodcuring tobaccobarns in steady windshake
of falling pines and blackgums. Slinging nasties with Paul's John Deere *putting* between

barn and field, wheels roll, spin–

a note in Obedience's diary: *July knows the withers of mules like the back of her hand*
and the drinkbottlecaps Clay nails to the bagging of the drags to hold the tobacco leaves.

George William Stephenson

I

Greatgreatgrandpap George's grandson—I called him Grandpa William—was born
  of Martha Johnson and Manly Stephenson, on the farm of "badlybent" George,
  off state road number 1517 in Pleasant Grove, Johnston County, North Carolina.
As a boy William hired himself out to Deb Wood to cut wood;
  helped his Uncle Naz, mauling and splitting rails
  and hauling them home.
He picked cotton,
  pulled corn, tended garden, raised goats, too,
  hogs aplenty snuffling paths harder when he'd pass with slops for the trough,
  slipping in his boots on the hill.
He moved across Middle Creek to Polenta, crossed the creek on a footlog, walked paths
  through woods.
One dark night a goat jumped up,
  scaring the daylights out of him:
"If the goat had not bleated, I think I would have died."

II

July was born ninety-eight years before I was.
Grandpa William was sixtyseven that year—1938.
He split wood for thirty cents a cord.
Got tired of helping Naz maul and haul those gums.
Hunted wild turkeys, rabbits, and squirrels.
Set traps in the swamps, catching anything he could: otter, mink, raccoon—
  one hide brought a dollar.
A yea and nay man.
Couldn't read or write.
Joined the church and started preaching.

And Grandmuh read the Bible to Grandpa every night.
Grandpa would listen, for he couldn't read or write.
He couldn't read or write.

You know that families moved in with one another back yonder,

a kind of underpinning: Manly and Martha with William and Nancy.
Martha had a skip she learned in Polenta.
Nancy joined the church in 1910.

Nancy

I

Grandmuh Nancy leans on her elbow: *oh my infantile paralysis—*
she purses her lips,
that indexfinger in the middle,
her hair in a bun
a splintery look's not yet ruint.
From her Bible and Old Baptist hymnals
she teaches you to read and write.
She dreams that you will sing for her when she is gone:

II

April 1, 1923

Dear July—

> *I wrote you a short letter Dec. 4th, 1922, but never mailed it. I only wrote for relief of mind with no intention of sending it to you then. Again I have a desire to write you, trusting that it is of the Lord that prompts the same.*
> *I will try to tell you the dream I had about you. If I mistake not it was the week before the 4th Sun. in July. I dreamed we were in a church house. It was communion and footwashing time. You and I were sitting together. You asked me to "take off your shoes and stockings that we might wash each other's feet." Oh, how unworthy I felt. Words cannot express my feelings. For years I had a desire to wash your feet, but I had always felt so little and unworthy I could not ask you and at last this happy privilege was mine! In silence I meditated. As I took off your stockings I saw there was a hole in your left one large enough that your whole heel was bare. This troubled me. And I thought if only I had a new pair of stockings I would give them to you to wear to the yearly meetings. I wished that I had some good enough for you. We washed each other's feet and I awoke. This dream troubled me.*
> *Finally it came to me this morning: I do not have to know what our dream means. I offer it to you for what it is worth, along with my love.*

Nancy

You and Greatgrandpa Manly picked blackberries
down near the edge of the woods
in front of the Old Place
and Manly stirred up some wasps
and those things *wrapped me up*
and stung me around my eyes.
Mister Manly chewed some Picnic Twist
and put some of the juice on my stings.
Then he took his pocketknife and picked the redbugs off me.

Playing Off One Another

I

Remember Doc Baker, July?
See him walking toward the Old Place: "Howdy, howdy, Mister Paul."

"You better not bat your eyes, Doc Baker, You took my ham.
Walk straight across that field by the Peter Place and never come back again."

Daddy: *I counted my hams every day and at dinner time I counted eight instead of nine.*
I always held some money back and didn't pay up complete; I didn't pay him no more.
Doc started walking home and I went up in the loft
          and there my ham was—under some fodder.
He was coming back to get it later.

I found that somebody got in our biscuitsafe in the kitchen, too, and had eaten some food.
I saw Ira, Doc's father.
He started talking ahead of hisself.

"Doc knows I don't whoop britches. I whoops meat."

I didn't law him.

One time Doc stole a cow from Cyrus Coats.

II

"Sun and moon gone down. . . ":
Fannie Abrams sang when she come to the Old Place to do the wash.
She was a big woman with a big belly.
Lived near the Beaver Dam bridge below Paul Coats's in a house owned by Will Long.
Lived there with Mac and Mary, mules, and carriages.
Other families, not quite so well off, would come work and take pay in hog's head.
For ten cents sometimes Pa would let them dig up a "lightered" stump.
We called Penny Bolling, Aunt Penny.
She was Percy's mother.

Aunt Pen married a Sanders the first time.
The Sanders children: Possum, Arthur, Richmond, Tabor,
          Hubert, Molly (Big Sis) and Marshline.
All these people used to work for Ma and Pa.
Pip Fellers, too, who fathered a lot of children.
His boys pulled fodder in season.
The girls helped with chores around the house.

III

Pip Fellers worked for the Johnson Boys across the creek,
lived in a rambly, shackly, unpainted shanty
grown over by sweetgum and honeysuckle
there right to the left of the old Sanders Place
where Lewis Sanders lived
telling me how there were bloodstains—
slave blood—on the railing going up stairs.

IV

You'd look over at the Family Graveyard
where the slaves lay, unmarked,
and wonder where you came from.

The furrows beached up rolls of clods,
ridged hate, ridged forget.
The years brought relief.

Nodding in the slow and steady switch
of the lines on the mule's back,
Pip learned not to break down.

Identity wrenched from your soul,
the end and beginning were the rows
he turned around.

V

When you consider the story, the bare fact
that we had little to offer ourselves; when you consider how
your family, July, would come Monday mornings wanting a job to do,

my father saying I have no money to pay
you with but I can swap you some eggs or meat for your
work; when you consider how snuff seemed to be the "city"

feel and taste on tongues inside lower lips; when you
consider the balance we achieved rarely, busting out often to
get drunk, fight, cutting one another in the face, of all places,

asking Daddy or my older brother Paul to Quick take me to the
Mergency Room; when you consider the little babies on pallets as
the women and grandparents picked our cotton; when you consider

the little bees in the honeysuckle sucking
the blossom, the big bees getting the honey,
the little man working the crops, the big man getting the money—

remembrance moves in the tone surrounding a dinner bell
far from a shanty, rings in the table full of September
peas, sidemeat, souse, sweet tomato wine!

VI

A swamp disorderly orders,
grassy briars and scrubgrowth
gone to meaning in a brusharbor of churchgoers
the creekbed perfect for the footwashings
you there in a silk dress lifting

for the water into which steps the preacher,
beads on your forehead
going under, breaking off illusion,
the conjured closeness

rushes
welcome through nearness unexpected.

VII

Aaron Langdon worked the Durham tobacco market.
The buyers graded Daddy's tobacco *wet.*
Aaron said government bought it,
      telling Daddy to take the tags off, since it was sold.
Daddy didn't budge.
Told Paul, Jr., and Aaron to get behind a post
      and he would talk to the American Tobacco Company buyer.
They did—and that tobacco brought 20 cents per pound more.
I can hear Daddy say: *This tobacco's not wet.*
I just didn't have a pit to bring it in order and I sprayed it a little.
Aaron Langdon said nobody but Paul Stephenson could do that!
His uniform was that Stetson.

VIII

Caterpillars
muscling up in arches
on the leaves, balls
caught in webs; Daddy, Percy, and I
among the yellow smell
taking the tobacco off the sticks,
Daddy, head down, bundling the leaves:
"You'll get ringworms, boy, go get some shoes on."

A thin lull of work
keeps us in that swell of time,
longbench, sticks in holes to separate the grades,
Daddy by the window, a cigar hanging in his mouth,
lost in thought on a foxrace,
his dogs lying on the pitdoor: Tony with white hairs
over his eyelids like an old man's winter, grim and profuse,
Butler yawning and yearning to run a rabbit in Beaver Dam,

Percy, snuffcontented, easing around the room.

IX

I will show you how I see it: Percy some time in the dark
coming down the long corn middles between
our shanty and the Old Place where he lived
squatting down by the right rear tire

sitting there screwing off the lugnuts
swinging the tire up over his shoulder
on the way out seeing the packhouse door to the hams
he had hung up on the sweetgum poles to cure

took one and went on across the field to Daddy's
boyhood home, now Percy's
bulging with sleep and transgressions

as the morning mounted again
outside the window
Daddy rising, never using the backhouse—that
was for sissies—went out behind the barn to nature's bidding
pausing at the shed to admire his Model-T
and saw the tire gone

not missing a breath in his ritual
went to church and waited for Percy to report to work on Monday:
"Percy, you took my tire, I know you did and don't you deny it."
"No sir, Mr. Paul, I sure didn't, but I know who did."
"And when you bring it back I want you to walk the road,
don't tote it through the field
and bring it in the daylight, not in the dark—and

bring my ham back, too, what's left and
sit down there and put the tire on and come with me
to the lowground and let's clear up them stumps."

24

"Yes sir"—and that was all; the tire
rolled on the car and "Mr. Paul"
bought his white Stetson later.

X

Daddy—and Rose's Holly—made a seine out of chicken wire.
The thing was so big they left it in the water and walked back home.
"We'll rake in the fish," Daddy said,
        "Horsefish at the Peter Hole big as yearlings."
He took two bamboo poles—big ones Mr. Willie Stephenson gave him—
        tying them together, making a hoop.
Uncle Reuben swapped him the wire for a bushel of cottonseed.
Holly and Daddy dragged that contraption to Middle Creek.
Wouldn't fit in the Peter Hole!
Looked like a turkey's waddle the water tried to swaller—
        as waller's to wallow: *I might be too old to cut the mustard,*
        but I shoregod can waller hit down?

Shepherd Said

My legs have give out.
I get the budgies, just can't stay in the house the way Liney can.
Me and her married, 1912, lived in Vasper Stephenson's house,
       near Retha Johnson's, and then at the Lamb Lassiter place.
The June Peter house was next, where we made twenty bales of cotton one year.
Me and Liney and the younguns picked a bale a day.
Leeman was born on the Lamb Land, Ruby at Jeems Parrish's
       where Hubert and Lucy lived.
Jut dated Beatrice Wallace; almost married her.
       Claude Honeycutt built the Old Place House where your father Paul and
       our family grew up.

Everyone's gone I used to run with.
Grandpa Manly once owned the Jeems Parrish home.
Manly give away all he had, it seems, after he come back from The War.
If someone needed a hog for meat and couldn't pay,
       he'd give the family his prize Duroc and make the box to cart it.

July mostly slept on a shucktick in her cabin.
Our bodies felt featherbeds.
She could heat a flatiron in a open fire
       and press our clothes like they were done up at a laundry.

Remember Uncle Bud and Aunt Florence?
Elsie—married their son, Lloyd—has been sick forever.
Lloyd loved Elsie until the whole world rang from his slickbacked
       hair to the polished workshoes.
When he stopped farming he walked his lines in his mind, never budging from stoveeyes,
       wore pinstriped overalls, smoked Sir Walter Raleighs, the newspaper,
       neatly creased, TVpage, face up.

One time Baldy, your grandpa William's brother, fell out of bed—or, rather,
       his wife Bet kicked him out.
Baldy said, "Darling you're going to break ever bone I got."
William was lying in the chimney outside, listening.

Bet put the latch on the door and they couldn't get in.
They'd been on a spree, Baldy saying he was going "irregardless of what Bet said,"
    because he wanted "to see a devilish bar."

II

One day I was in Four Oaks, on the street there,
Saw Jim, the chicken-eating mule, tied to a tree.
Sam Poor, an old black man, come back to get him,
and I said, "Where'd you get your mule."
"From a Hodges man near Benson."
The old man had some groceries and some Carolina's Best flour in his buggy.
Jim had eat his flour and strowed it all over and I knew it was the mule
        Pa bought from J. S. Barbour in Clayton when I was four years old.
Jim was five when Pa bought him.
The man said he traded a "hoss" for Jim, said he bought him for a eleven-year old mule.
I know for sure he was at least thirty.
All the boys in our family plowed him, except Walter.

III

Liney keeps blinking how she and Shep
        married at Jim Zack Jones's house, March 30, 1912.
She was sixteen, going on seventeen; he was seventeen, going on eighteen.
"Paul's content to stay home and Shepherd can't be still, going everywhere forever,
        without being nowhere: Shep's tied down, because of me:
        he won't go out of hearing of this room."

IV

She will die first, Shep said.
I am ninetytwo.
Liney is ninety.

She is in this resthome
and I am in another.

I visit her like I'm doing now.

Last night in the shape of a dream
she was on a plane going toward heaven
and I was on another right behind her.
You wait and see what I tell you.
Until then I say a little prayer.
She looks like she's asleep.

I know she knows what I say because we
have been married for seventyfive years.
You don't have to say nothing after that long.

Greatgrandpa Manly

> *– STEPHENSON, MANLY, Private. Resided Johnston County, by occupation
> a farmer prior to enlisting in Johnston County at age 28, October 3,1862, for The War.
> Reported present in November-December, 1862, and September, 1863-February, 1864.
> Also reported present in July-August and November-December, 1864. Co. D, 50th
> Regiment N.C. Troops. Survived The War* (North Carolina Troops, 1862-1865: A Roster,
> Compiled by Weymouth T. Jordan, Jr., Vol. XII, Infantry, 49th-52nd Regiments,
> Raleigh, North Carolina, Division of Archives & History, 1990, 195).

I

There—in the Nimrod Stephenson Memorial Cemetery—
fought at Drury's Bluff on the James River, below Richmond,
organized into a brigade made of regiments
and the 2nd Battalion North Carolina troops (in all about 2, 200)
with Brigadier General Junius Daniel in command.
Near Darkesville, Virginia, July 21, 1863,
General Daniel turned over command to Colonel Edmind C. Brabble.

II

"Grandpa Manly learned me a sense of history; that is all I know now—or need to know,"
my father said. He settles on Manly's shoulders. They walk over "the plantation,"
what's left after the battle.

III

You knew the sounds of rifles being cocked,
speculators you hoped would not feel your arms and legs,
ask questions about your health.

Your children, unrecognized, worked the land,
a daughter, growing, coming to a master

will I be beaten
will I be sad–
will he see me tenderly
when I close my eyes?

Barbours

James N. Barbour, Private: father of my father's mother.
Name's on the Roster of North Carolina Troops.
A Johnstonian tanner, he enlisted in Northampton County, May 1861.
A teamster, he sounded the detail.
Paroled, May, 1865, he came back home—alive—leaving his cousin Ruffin on the field.
No more the bugle calls the weary one; rest, noble spirit, in a grave unknown.

II

You are the world you were born to, July.
Out of your house, footdust, shuckmouse on a cob,
        your voice ghosting the husk pain gnaws—
        some shanty in Pleasant Grove with cracks
        so wide you can see the biddies scratching.
Your own featherbed—a present from Obedience Stephenson—indents a room
        warm with woodcrackle, eaves hung with icicles, dreams under seven quilts,
        trees in your temples, enough branches in your ears after Reconstruction to make
        a reindeer rut.

You eye the dusty ditches, when days come lean, obscure,
        for slavery's real as the scum you wash off every night.

III

I lose you, July, in names on granite, the *shall* and *will* leveling the plain:
        out of the lows a crawling goes, crumbs under a plate,
        signs of you between the lines,
        punctuating highs wedded to weep and know ecstasy withers,
        heaves, disappears,
        then tunes finale the curtain, certain, separates, mocks.

Those warring Barbours!
Mystery of the cousin's grave, his identity lost as yours, July, in the war's afterbirth:
        white rage riding the countryside, the prancing hooves the cavalry charges:

31

human chattel, manifold events, poised forward, back, gravelly shapes.

Some Native Americans must have succumbed down around the Persimmon Tree Hole,
        on Middle Creek, the mounds there, signs,
            the scoopedout rock where they washed their wares they made with their hands.

Wherever they dug and planted, danced and slept, where the oxen afterward bore down
        muscles for the plow to break newground—
            the selfsame fields, July, you dreamed, picking up points the Indians made,
            their bones scattered in the dirt, cornstalks to mark their places.

Limbs haunt the corners of your cabin,
lifting bare feet ghosting
faces in oaktreeroots,
hovering shapes opening doors,

the graveyard craving no more
where your heirs rise as masters kneel,
the dream, outworn,
the people left forgetting
what went before.

Johnsons

I

My mother's mother, Auriba Westbrook Lee, married Marshall Perry Johnson
who, my mother said, tied a rope around a mulberry and one end to his neck—
      and jumped off.

      Her face in the photo seems rough,
      Caught in the glass
      Abruptly enough
      For me whose grief's a photograph.

      Paul, Jr., said
      She was behind the kitchen door
      When he got off the schoolbus—
      "Boo," she said. "I'm still trembling,"
      He said.

II

DADDY SAID: These Johnsons don't—and never—look where they are going.
Maytle couldn't walk for a long time.
Never went to a doctor.
Orron and his father had gone to town on a cart
      and got back about dark to find her sprawled in wheat straw.
She was about five years old—had jumped off the roof of a shed into the pile
      and stuck a splinter in her thigh, there on that farm
      sixty acres cross the road on the church side
      and seventy on the side with the house.
      Orron said his father lay in the hallway
      of that house in Elevation Township before the funeral.
All the family went to the burial in a buggy,
      Mr. Benny Coats hauling him by wagon down to the old home
      near Meadow—at Peacock's Crossroads.

ORRON: My father died in 1913, February 12.
I found him, near the hogpen, hanging by a rope tied over a mulberry limb.
I was waiting for the schoolbus.

33

Mother sent me to check on him.
I was eleven years old.
I remember Billy Flowers, Roscoe's father, coming to the house
       and talking to the people that day.
In front of an open fire the women served peeled oranges on a plate.

The Last Breath

The mulberry looks ornamental,
its trunk irregular as Grandfather's mind,
the graygreen foliage total gray as the last breath leaves;
veins, threepronged, scroll up like a fiddlehead;
one limb, a horsehairbow saws his days,
soft headhairs, rough temples,
though none cushions him 12 February 1913,
the hardy branches, cold,
dangling dustmotions
the hogs kick up while February sings
haints, July, you know may never be gone for good,
the moss, a rock at my Grandfather Johnson's head, St. Mary's Grove.

II

You are the rounding
moon over rooftops, July,
crops, hackled feathers,
elves loose in corners,
that stranger rank as the ham my mother sliced to flush drunkardflies—
taint in the hum her lips pursed,
spirituals rising out of thickets and brambles where birds roosted in the woods.
I see you skipping, barefooted, way down in the fall, your instep, arched.

Shub Throws One Voice to Mama & Another to July

I

MAMA: When I was a little girl Vurtle and me used to go to my grandfather's and grandmother's house to spend a week. Vurtle and I would go spend a few days with them and Grandmama would take us with her to get up the eggs. The nests were on the ground under the shelter. She had a long stick with a dipper on the end. She could not stoop.

JULY: *When I was a little girl I was not strong enough to wring a pullet's neck. So I would get me a tobacco stick and lay it on the neck, place my feet on each end of the stick and pull the pullet's feet straight up until the neckbone snapped. I would keep pulling like that until the head fell off and the neck would spurt blood while the chicken danced round and round.*

MAMA: Before I was born Mama said something in a dream told her I would have a daughter and her name shall be Maytle Rose. And it was a girl! Aunt Sarah asked her (Auriba) what she was going to name me. She said I don't know—Maytle Rose, I reckon. Aunt Sarah said: Now, Orby, you haven't named a one after me. So to keep her from thinking hard she named me Maytle Samantha. Her name was Sarah Samantha. So later on in years I got married. Then our first child was born, a little girl.

JULY: *I was fishing then, clamoring on Swift Creek, Jart's old felt hat crouched like a fox on my head. I was dreaming among the watersnakes and gutted logs, poking my fingers into the narrow bower of a Prince Albert Crimp Cut can for a black and yellow catalpa worm to thread with a twig, wrongsideout, exposing the yellow meat for me a bream.*

I was born one morning in the month of my name and the clock was ticking on the mantel Ju-ly, Ju-ly.

MAMA: Someone went after Mama down there. When she got back, the little baby was born. Paul was sitting in the room with her in his lap. And Mama asked him: What are you going to name her, Paul? He said, I don't know, Maytle, I reckon. Mama said You put the Maytle and I'll put the Rose. So she had a Maytle Rose after all, after she dreamed it all.

JULY: *I was so old then I really was July, a girl again–forever. I know how to wait. Once upon a time they said I was 3/5ths of a person. I learned not to know something before it came along to me. Now I been knowing a long time.*

MAMA: And 4 ½ years later Paul, Jr., was born. His name had to be Paul, Jr. Then 7 years later Marshall came along. And we named him after Grandpa William and your Grandpa Marshall. Then 1 year and 7 days I had another little baby. So I was going to name it, if it was a girl, Shelby Jean, after a little girl, Shelby Jean Davis who sang on the radio, but when it was born, it was a boy. So Uncle Reuben said Name him Shelby Dean, after Dizzy. So here Shub is.

II

WILL YOU LOVE ME WHEN I'M OLD
for Shub–and July, too

Let me ask of you, my darling,
One question soft and low,
That gives me many a heartache,
As the moments come and go.

I had hoped that you would ask me,
That my blushes you would share,
But at last I have to ask you,
As so much for you I care.

I will ask of you this question,
If will not improper be.
It is only this, my darling,
Would you care to marry me?

Let me claim of you a promise,
Worth to me a world of gold.

37

It is only this, my darling,
Will you love me when I'm old?

When my hair shall shame the snowdrift
And my eyes will dimmer grow,
I will lean upon some loved one,
In the valley as I go.

Now these questions I have asked you,
And I hope you will forgive,
For I love you, little darling,
And I will as long as I live.
{I made this verse up.}

Wide and deep respect: J. Ford 1872
Copy written By
Maytle J. Stephenson (ha ha)

5-25-1965
Tune: "Rosewood Casket"

I Can See Clearly Now

I

My father talked of girls he courted: Mary Heath, Lula Barbour,
Pauline Neighbors, most of them from Barbour Town:

"I got a letter from Maytle, telling me her mother Orby said we were getting too serious
and Maytle was too young anyway and 'You better not come see me no more.'
That made me a little mad. I went to see another girl instead, late one day, and I passed
Maytle, walking the road, crying; I went back. Her mother said we might as well get
married, we were seeing so much of each other anyhow. I told Vurtle me and her might
have married, if her sister Maytle had not jumped up to get beside me every time Vurtle
got up."

II

Vurtle, Maytle, Rose—blushes—bushes.
Viburnam!

Naz, Pap George's son, took Penny Stancil, nicknamed Chilly, as his second wife.
Naz's and Pin's son, John, took morphine instead of Calamint.
Shep stayed with John's wife, Martha, to help keep John awake!
His brother, Ira, went after Dr. Mac who *come and give him a shot to make him throw*
> *up—trying to fall asleep, talking out of his head—*
> attempted escapes in logs scooped out to float like boats,
> death by drowning high in bottomlands—moccasins in the night—
lynchings, cuttings, carvings, hangings, whiskeydrinking!

III

The dark takes over: the window
sill shakes beyond the glass.
On the hill, Sam Poor and his
wife Annie Mae in a print dress
rip bloodpainting patterns,
flowers on that sack—

39

clawing body sweat through rye whiskey
breath he cocks a singletree he used to plow the mule.
On her knees she pleads don't kill me
Sammy

Better shut your mouth now, see

On Christmas eve
he hangs her to the tierpoles of his landlord's barn—
dangling on a frayed plowline under the roof's
eaves while the mule's broke rope
stays.

IV

     The first settlers wanted more; they took it,
     God's will be done, they said; the corruption they found,
     God Almighty's all along.
     Like a sour place at the back of the throat,
     violence erupted everywhere,
     the hurt and heartache, the headaches,
     seasons of shouting, scaring the neighbors,
     wondering how we got this way, July, wanting some rest
     so we might resist the burrowing-in blur of loneliness and mortality:

We cannot know much more about ourselves than the
configurations of entanglement and disentanglement—
the bloodletting in the backyard when the hired Hand
placed the rooster's neck on the block and said no more would he
chop the wood for the stove, no more would he leave the heads
with the open eyes lying on the ground for days, his clothes
smelling of urine and Sweet Peach Snuff, his spittle scattered:
       what getting here means sends the senses along a path
       of disorder, a miserable mountain of crises
       as if the youth in us does not exist to keep us young

but to breed a restlessness in our very knees,
conforming to the reckoning reconstruction of obstacles,
the sinking in to escape

     ripe, wrapping tobacco leaves leathery on the stalk,
     corn, tomatoes, potatoes, backbone, sidemeat, gravy,
     okra—faces of slaves—surface and inner core:

          hogkillings: the ground was frozen, then a thaw. It was a
          pure, endless time of scraping the hair off with Kerr jarlids,
          hanging the dressed hogs up to the gallows,
          stuffing the sausage, drying the lard and holding the bathed
          day in cold suspension.
          I used to run in and out under the hamstrung animals.
          The mere wonder brought pain.
          Moments reappeared in a totally absorbed stretch of
          footsteps and concerns, a rendering of boundless lessons.

That's the Way It Was

I

Oldtimey preachers promised sin.

Van Della, princess, bronzedskinned,
could string tobacco fast as handers could get it to her.
Swing her hips, too; the earth moved galaxies
above her widebrimmed straw,
lifting globes paradise might claim
as plumbing for plumage,
the most splendid single light grass could yield to,
her heels down, toes pointing those bare feet
quivering grains under the chaineytree,
sand cooling her toes as she approached the tobaccobench.

Leaning forward, I see you bring the blackening pot to a boil,
the garments turning spotless on the fluted washboard,
listening to what the white folks say, hearing your mother pray again,
        telling you, *July, wait and work – and once Freedom is declared –*
               don't make no crops beyond the time, no matter what, and run and tell other
               slaves they can quit work now they are free! No matter what!

II

Uncle Reuben told me *you* are doing good if you have enough money to buy
        fertilizer for next year's crop.
I told him Seth Woodall paid Pap George $413.25 for July, the slave girl, in 1850.
He and Aunt Mary farmed just twenty-two acres.
Everybody wanted poundage in tobacco.
We would heat a kettle on the stove and pour the scalding water in the stems.
Uncle Reuben would build a fire in the washpot and heat his water
and drib it on the stems of the cured tobacco to gain a little weight.
He could grin and stir up a little money.

Old Jim was Reuben's mule before Rhody.
Reuben traded him in for one younger.
Didn't you know him, July?
I admired his muleshoes.
I went barefooted year round.
Wintertime my feet cracked open.

I could really pick cotton.
I'd get in the field early in the morning:
        it weighed more when dew was on the bolls.
Even when my hands cracked open from the cold I kept on filling up my sack.
Me and Obedience would slip off to a sweet potato bank.
She told me a potato hill looked like a igloo.
I wondered where she'd seen one – I won't never forget that.
We'd build a fire and roast the white-fleshed batatas
        in the hot ashes and we'd sit and eat and warm our hands over the fire.
That was really living.

Aunt Mary, The Civil War, & New Orleans, 2005

I

I can hear her now:

One weekend spree
> Uncle Dray got drunk in the grapevine, his specs lost and false teeth hanging in
> the arbor, scuppernongbrandy waving inside his head and the tenacrefield
> needing plowing.

"How many eggs you want for breakfast, Dray?"

"I don't even want to see no chicken, Mary."

The white enamel bucket in the kitchen, the dented dipper in
> the wellbucket on the curb—a gourd floating twice in the water,
> the cow's milk and butter in another pail deep down in the well
> where the water's a little milky from a spill.
> Uncle Reuben's hands draw up the rope,
> a "refrigerator" bubbling the surface like a pot percolating.
Dipped Railroad Mills, splurging the water good; a brown roll ripples like cocoa.
Aunt Mary didn't dip unless she walked.
She was a thinking woman.
Her Stephenson face pearshapes,
> peering out around the curtains she sewed for her windows in the kitchen,
> the cardinal piping stitched leftovers from an apron she made,
> hands brushing her dress to rest.
Dinnerbell rings two shakes.

II

My Mary's mad at rest.
The granite stone cannot say she had spells.
Fanning the briars around her hair,
> we buried her at Rehobeth in the hazed spring sun rising in a circle,
> rabbits nibbling sugarcakes she made until the last dress she owned
> someone else ironed and laid clean, no telling she had migraines.

Temples flared, her flat, addled words would not dare
　　　　say a doctor miles away in town might give her some relief,
　　　　Primitive as she was.
Let Fate try scare the faith she had.
Like a lover, he might tease her headaches back,
　　　　a sign she was not meant to live long,
　　　　lest her husband say he'd decided to wire the house for electricity,
　　　　take her for a drive in his roadster, buy her an icecreamcone.

III

In 1865
　　　　there went out a Proclamation into the future
　　　　　　　　Freedom marched North and South in colors
　　　　　　　　　　　　lining roads and fields you ran
　　　　　　　　　　　　　　　　dodging patrol through plantations
　　　　　　　　　　　　　　　　　　　　braving the whip winging your feet

struggling every inch the land
　　　　and up the creeks and rivers where seines bottomed out
　　　　　　　　crouching and singing
　　　　　　　　　　　　What child shall enter the kingdom?

One lamplight in your window
　　　　dangles on braiding wound in golden threads you jump to touch.

All American

– 11 Jan. 1850: George Stephenson of Johnston County, guardian to heirs
of Jacob T. Woodall, deceased, sells to James G. Woodall of Johnston County for $241.00
a negro boy Clay ca. 7 yrs. Wit: Gideon & William Woodall.
Signed: George Stephenson, Feb. Ct., 1851. (Kinfolks, Volume II, 116).

I

Don't let the Help go free–
if they are not guilty in time they will be–
America, Yankee, Venus, Marzilla, Sarah,
July, Clay–the Family Graveyard
where the slaves' graves spread dying,
rocks for stones unmarked and rained on
all these years, my father saying:

Your greatgreatgrandpap George
and here his slaves
I should remember. . .

July, they say your dance was sorrowful
because you had fanfeet:
Roasting potatoes in a brushheap
with my runaway husband,
I vowed to live with him in Finch's Mash forever.
Then came the patterrollers. . . he to his captain's farm. . .
me to my place . . . like mules.

Girls with strong, pretty legs whose feet pointed straight brought more money.

II

A canoe slips through cattails and elms in the Great Dismal Swamp thick with bluetailed
rabbits. Runaway slaves escaped here. *One time July put black pepper in her socks to*
make the hounds sneeze, throw them off her track. Mr. Robert Vinson's seated in a
kitchen chair, his wife Velma behind in one, too, paddling the homemade boat as calmly

as they would sit in the back pew at church, fog enveloping moss on the elms,
the stumpy trunks of cypresses near the water like preachers out of pulpit.

III

Obedience had a neighbor named Ada, rawboned woman at the end of a long
path, always heartbroken, face scrubbed to redden outlook wherever she was,
sort of stumbled when she walked, her sweater camouflaging a voice of
maroon banter, leaving her Howdies up in the air. Ada's eyes shined her teeth.
Once a week she'd take a kettle of hot, scalding water and wash down the walls
of her plankhouse, pouring a dipperful down the bedposts to kill the silverfish;
chinches would crawl out of that dark fold where the mattress lapped the sides
and the ticking collapsed into itself.

1886: July: *My bedroom filled with chinches. They got so bad I tried everything. I got
myself a pallet and put it in the middle of the floor and poured molasses around it. A few
younguns got stuck, but them big red dark chinches crawled up the walls to the center of
the ceiling and fell down on me on that pallet. Then I saw an ad in a broadside at the
commissary: Sure Cure for Chinches. What I got was a block and a mallet and what it
said was, "Put bedbug on block, hit hard with hammer." "That'll work," I said to
myself, "if I can live long enough."*

IV

Clee stands on Paul's Hill,
looking up at the man's face, the boss who does not fall or fail
after Lincoln frees the slaves, Clee's home in the big house the boss
moves out of after The War
so that now the two men
together face each other, the one
taller on the steps of his new brick house than the
other standing in the yard,
crossing his busted brogans,
making marks in the dirt,
the tall man answering the other:
>   *Naw, I shore ain't, Clee,*
>   *you might try Mr. Heck*
>   *up the road yonder, he might have some work.*

The Roll Call of Tenants

I

In the howling light, July, 11 January, 1850, the lonely weather rolls the blues from Henry Knight's lips, his left hand sliding the bottleneck up the strings; behind him Stephen Foster's darkies rise up out of the laps of their masters, saying you will be in

our humanity this time: we will live together as children and grow old remembering the planked floors baring cracks, doors open wide from your kitchen to worlds outside, flies buzzing from backdoor screens to live in rank rapport, waiting for legislatures to set

society spinning with the earth's unspeaking tongues patterns and elements primary as the routes the tenants, black and white, take from my birthplace, your home by Middle Creek, central as the old painter Thaddeus told, always yesterday, when he

remembers playing in his yard, some resistance to pain joy carries around in a sling so ragged words won't come out of our undernourished "children" we grew up with: I see you down the hill in the clay, digging with spoons: you put it in a

washbasin and walk strong to the tenant house where you smell the baked clay as much as a blackberry pie you pick later, and the clay and pie together will be a treat you never know better: we stand and wait and Duck hums a shroud or scarf of a

sound out of the sawbriars on the bank: I wonder and know I can never shake the experience there, Duck moaning and saying, Shub, sing me a song and I always sing about peace, angels, lambs, and black nights like the sea: oh we are young in our need

for the earth to let us be—tenants—white and black: Marshall Brown, wife Eloise, daughter Annie Mae; A. Z. James (drinks himself to death before his suicide); Clee Tarry, a strong man who can lift a stick of green tobacco and muscle it straight out, first,

then stick it up to the hangers on the tierpoles, and his wife Lucy; Elvis Tarry, wife Mae Dinah (whose feets always hurt), her sister, Molly (who looks like a man and wears a man's worn-out brogans); June Williams and wife Viola and children, Moonkey,

Russell, David, Billy (Viola lives in a stupor three out of seven—thin as a stick, she and June drink Oblivion); Roof and Thelma Allen. Like A. Z., Roof kills himself: I know June best: He carves his initials in the crown of the chimney of our "new" house, built

1952: I take a shower in the basement when June comes down the outside stairs and sees me and I turn my backside to him and he says, "Shub, I got one too": Minnie Birch picks cotton and she wears a sack dress which falls in folds over her stomach:

she and Duck and Lil Sis come to the hill to dig the clay: and there is Henry Knight and his wife Mary, their children and grandchildren, Henry playing the blues every which way; sometimes he bars the strings with his pocketknife: I lie down and

listen for you to note what summer brings to the four separate entrances for moviegoers at the theatre in Red Springs, North Carolina, one for the whites, one for the blacks, one for the Indians, and one for the Smilies who, somebody said, didn't know who they were.

II

The earth encloses us in a sea of faith; darkness fills again; across Sanders Road in the old Stephenson cemetery, you and the other slaves, still, without markers, anonymous as the dirt, the hedges, fallen, wirefences growing into the treetrunks, you,

seeing what you saw: a foster child helps a man work on a car, the man watching that child grow up, growing her up until they can wait no more, setting out tobacco at night in May, the long rows, the two untangling the plants and *sometimes they'd be thirty*

minutes gone down the moist rows, the transplanter smoothing the ridges, the plant going in, gush of water and the work getting done, the child having the baby while the man fumed that he was going to "get that Banks boy" who done wrong.

III

Jad, Conroe, Lula Morgan, Molly, Lil Sis! Jad, amasser of a grin, hammockshaped, swinging a swath wide and silent enough to jar any man or woman: he must have been six-ten and the way he carried his head made him giraffe-like, dignified under

a too-small Sunday hat: *didn't drink or smoke*, just smiled and grinned and lilted and when I would go to his house to get him to help work he was always ready: lived with his wife, no children, had plenty of money he saved toward salvation and he *brought a little piece of cheese and a cracker wrapped up in newspaper in his bib-*

overalls and one time he and Conroe helped brother Paul cut some gums out of the
branch, working all day long, and Jad would eat his cheese and cracker, Conroe sitting

among the stumps, his jowls hanging full of potted meat and crackers, his eyes black
olives left out of oil, little red, like a dog's, not like a man's at all *and he had a Pepsi bottle
filled with turpentine, a tuft of green pineneedles stuffed in the top–a sprinkler!*

He'd dash some drops on the blade of the crosscutsaw: *"I knows what I
knows and I been knowing it."*

IV

Lula Morgan never bought a pole to feel the limber swish of a channel cat run like a
young shoat down the creek: for her sweetgum would do: she'd take her pocketknife
and shave the knots off the limb, the line seeking itself exactly as the crookedness would

not hinder the way she sat on the bank waiting for the *dobdobdob* of the horsefish,
bottomfeeder that he is or the quick swoosh the crackershell makes, no matter: she was a
washwoman there to catch a little meal for the table.

V

And there was Molly: *overalls with bottomless pockets, loppedover man's brogans,
big cheeks, plaited hair, face round-settling into a cottonmiddle Septembers, her cottonsack
caking with a layer of thin mud–one of those big, fat, green horny worms does

not bother her. On the evening of the third day of picking cotton she said she'd quit, too
old (she had picked 400 pounds a day) she'd take to washing and ironing for white
women who could afford some payment.*

VI

Lil Sis and July, body and soul–one motion–tall, lanky, skin bronze, muscular–eyes
darting as they come across the field from the Old Place, long legs, the way they
put the hedge between themselves and my world, gone, disappearing as easily as they

50

come, growing up fast as they had to—the wild, lost look of wonder, not
harmony, pretty life, primitive, a sad iron to rub over their few pieces of
clothing, God's load carried, the family farmed out, looked after,

nevertheless, helped along by some place to go into their resonance, their
loose, gangly touches braided between cornfields and tobaccopatches, specters
dissolving in the heat, July expressing herself to this girl

coming like her own self around the bend.

VII

Millard, barefooted, a little man dressed in bluebibbed overalls,
looks everywhere for a way out of conversation to sing
"In That Great Getting-Up Morning," shouting *Mahalia!* –
sometimes hushing for a minute or so to tell July how times would change
the mesh of primers goosestepping the tobacco middles FLAP right hand under the left,
the going-around-the-stalk-handful of tobacco tucked in the pit of the off-arm,
Millard's songs coming out refracted in the bushwet green weeds
he'd walk through to get to the end of the rows,
just get to the end of the row, he says, *That's all she wrote.*

VIII

Fare thee well workers wail from the fields—
corn, cotton, tobacco, peas,
spirituals of Hands working together in the cold and the heat—
hoe
ho
hay
hey
how
they hoe the rows
make haymows
stacks of strawlike
haystacks
you got to walk that Lonesome Valley

hymns jostling rags,
head blooming sweat. . .
belief one thing,
beef, another; goose
and the gander's at hand
under the swamp bay
freeing feathers:
You work your fingers to the bone and get bony fingers.

IX

You have walked from the tobaccofields to the road,
a quarter
mile to Mr. Roberts's Store,

shuffling around there close to the hoopcheese
until he says If you're not careful
you're going to fall on my cheese:
you hear Duck let out that closedlipped smile,
laughing a little for grace
since she won't open her mouth
because the Sweet Society she's dipping might dribble out

and you go ahead,
guarding your hunger, longing for something,
maybe some tenderloins
in the back meat counter, saying what he knows you will, unknotting your rag—
"Can I please have a can of 'pottish' meat and a box of soda crackers?"

The Refrain

I

2008: In a box (PC 330 *Sanders*) at the Heritage Center, Smithfield, North Carolina, there is a history of a place. The hand, a cursive quill, marks Baldy Sanders, his slaves, totaling 128, starting, 1785, ending, 1865. Sampler:

AGES OF MY NEGROES WHEN BORN AND DIED   /   DEATHS OF MY NEGROES

Amy, born 1785

Mourning, born August 11, 1823

Rose was born   *Died in the fall of 1836*

America, born April 14, 1833, sold to John C. Moore, August 16, 1850

Israel was born August 1, 1833   *Died July 30, 1835*

Julia was born July 27, 1845.

Washington was born February 23, 1851   *Smothered January 18, 1852*

Francis was born October 28, 1858   *Died March 21, 1863 of Scarlet fever*

Anaca was born December 28, 1860   *Anaca Died June 12, 1861*

Vina was born December 28, 1860   *Vina Died July 12, 1861*

February 6, 1861 (Old Nancy) Died. Supposed to be 100 years old or more. Died about 7 o'clock A.M.

King was born August 23,1861

Ann was born January 25, 1865

Another America was one of the 143 Watson slaves—"& 13 increase"—sold in 1861 (*Kinfolks*, Vol. II, 169, 179).

Soon there would be no push
      through underbrush
            hiding places in Finch's Mash
                  pineknot flares
                     chattel
                         like cattle
                             meeting
                                 debts
                                   with deaths
no more nails in barrels
      rolling slaves
            ships leaking and dipping in the twisting Neuse
             refuse
                 abuse
                     shivering alone on the banks of the river
                          named for the Tribe of the Neusiok.

III

L. H. Sanders's slaves listed in a column beside George Stephenson's Seven,
the L. H. Sanders slaves, evaluated, 1863, at $13,850, to dwell on the plantation of Baldy
Sanders (L. H.'s father): Ben, Betsy, Bill, Delaney ("deformed"), Doctor, Gracy, Isaac
("infirm: fits"), Israel, Jane, Jim, Jo ("unsound"), Laney, Larkin, Lef, Martha, Marzilla,
Minney, Penny, Richmond, Rosety, Silvy, Tempy, Tinnett, Warren, Wash, Westley (the
carpenter), Westley (again), Wiley, Wilson.

July and Clay together: *Sarah, Haywood, Marzilla,*
Venus, Daniel, Silvy, Jart–

That refrain in your head's inviolate, July.
You close your eyes and blink hard when the sun goes down.

The way you move,

carrying a basket of laundry on your head,

bending your knees to glide and lilt like Venus
lowering your apron to spoon hen-eggs out of the hedge,

your pride the fleecy stars—
before our eyes close, milky and mattered,

shall decency's calling be—
future's sunup

returning home, nights: light the lamp,
sit in the shanty's door, sweep the dirtfloor,

fall asleep with the chickens on the roostpoles,
rise with them, over and over, feathers, yielding to grass

feet bend down, hearts crying out against the highest bidder,
the planters, buckled to bigger yields.

IV

Will your family leave this spot
for what's beyond The Hill
or die here with gum on your hands?
Tierpoles swell and squeak for feet.
Hand that tobacco down.
Your greatgreatgrandson, Clee,
stops at the barn
just long enough to let me
know he is not
going to climb the tierpoles;
looks like a treetrunk
standing in the door:
turtleshell, domeshaped
hard hat,
tightened lips;
never speaking

he stands there on the sandy bottom of the barn,
three men—one on the top rack of tiers, one
below, and Clee on the ground in his cutoff shirt,
that right arm like a hog's ham,
his nostrils flaring, poking the bulky stick of green tobacco
up to the man on the lower tierpoles—
a look of pure displacement
as if the sky were a roofdome
and the dirt beneath his feet
might move mountains.

Coffin, Seeds, Inventory

—Account Sale: By amount paid: N. B. Honeycutt:
Coffin: Oct. 19, 1886: $12.50 (from Accounts of Sale of George Stephenson,
filed May 29, 1886, Nazareth Stephenson & M. J. Langdon, Executors,
recorded in Record of Accounts No. 4, Pages 211 to 214).

I

Greatgreatgrandpap George was so bowbacked
they could hardly get him in his coffin.
He was buried in the field with "his" slaves,
my father, his greatgrandson Paul in that Stetson
playing his banjo the clawhammerstyle
gold glinting in his teeth
oh my darling Nellie Gray
they have taken you away
thirtyfive dogs *Atlas Bing Bob Butler Cora*
Fanny Fancy Ginger Lula Belle Ringwood
Sing Slobber Mouth Sounder Tony Music
all would cross the Stephenson Cemetery
the unmarked graves—July—
nothing but creekrocks at your heads.

II

According to waking
live
rise and fall—
walking stick,
trowel, hammer,
auger and bit,
smoothing irons, grappling knives,

cow, calf, saw, frying pan,
meat box, pitcher, featherbed, testament, hymn book,
history, old books, umbrella, trunk, bed and contents,

bedstead, mattress, lard, geese and four chickens—
shovel—and you—

July—head back,
your frayed sleeves sliding over a vine:
It's about cooking time.
My country! Be still! Hush!

Photograph by Jan G. Hensley

Shelby Stephenson grew up on a small farm near Benson, in the Coastal Plain of North Carolina. After leaving the farm for college, he graduated from the University of North Carolina-Chapel Hill (where he also studied law), University of Pittsburgh, and the University of Wisconsin-Madison. He is professor of English at the University of North Carolina-Pembroke, where he has edited *Pembroke Magazine* since 1979. The state of North Carolina presented him with the 2001 North Carolina Award in Literature. He has received the Zoe Kincaid Brockman Memorial Award, North Carolina Writers' Network Chapbook Prize, Bright Hill Press Chapbook Award, and the Brockman-Campbell Poetry Prize. In addition to *Family Matters: Homage to July, the Slave Girl*, he has published a poetic documentary *Plankhouse* (with photographs by Roger Manley), *Middle Creek Poems, Carolina Shout!, Finch's Mash, The Persimmon Tree Carol, Poor People, Greatest Hits, Fiddledeedee,* and *Possum.* With his wife Linda he has made three musical CDs *Hank Williams Tribute; Stephenson Brothers & Linda Sing the Old Songs; When Country Was Country.* Shelby and Linda live on the farm where he was born.